Waders, Wind Knots & Wooly Boogers

By John Fuhrman

Business Lessons Learned on The Fly

DreamHouse
Publishing
www.dreamhousepublishing.com

DreamHouse *Publishing*

2100 Blossom Way South
St. Petersburg, Fl 33712

Copyright© 2004 John Fuhrman

ISBN 0 - 9755516 - 0 - 4

Printed in the United States of America.

**Special discounts on bulk quantities are
available from DreamHouse Publishing.
Contact:
dreamhouseorders@hgml.net**

Cover Art:
Trout Stream by James M. Sessions (1882-1962)

Dedicated to my family. To Helen, John, and Katie. Your laughter, love and confidence are the examples I need to finish my mission.

Contents

"Never let the opinions of someone else control your thoughts and actions."

Introduction

Fly-fishing. Isn't that an expensive hobby for snobs and elitists who use required skill as an excuse for not being able to catch fish?

Those thoughts and others like them had set the course my life had taken until someone put a fly rod in my hand and made me try it. It was at that very moment that I learned one of life's most valuable lessons. *Never let the opinions of someone else control your thoughts and actions.*

For years I had scoffed at those who went off to hike the streams and rivers with oversized rods and microscopic insect looking things that you have to tie yourself (or you're not really a sincere sportsman) as they "hunted" the elusive trout.

As with broccoli in the past, I felt certain I didn't have to try luring fish to strike a minute collection of yarn, feathers, and hooks tied together to know that I certainly wouldn't enjoy it. And to top it off, I lived with those thoughts well into my thirties. Even though by then I was enjoying cream of broccoli soup in the fall, fresh broccoli for dipping at a raw salad bar, and cooking it several ways as it has become my favorite vegetable.

I'm not here to share with you or even suggest that if you try fly-fishing you'll become devoted to it. In fact, I'd prefer if you didn't. Part of the pleasure is drawn from the existing solitude due to the fact that not many participate, and my hope is that situation will remain. I've grown to enjoy it for many reasons that have little to do with the desired end result. That's what this book is all about. I want to give you a look at what I've learned while casting on the different waters for the last thirty days.

Initially, I set out to reward myself with thirty days of fishing the streams and rivers that I had only been able to enjoy one weekend at a time. I wanted to be able to become better at the sport than previously limited trips would allow. When you only have a couple of days, the object is to catch fish – any way you can. Over a period of thirty days, catching no longer is a priority; getting better is. However, the trip provided me much more.

I was able to discover more about business, life, and especially what makes me what I am than at any other period in my nearly fifty-odd years on this planet. I don't pretend to have all the answers to life's puzzles. Perhaps for some of you I have no answers at all. But I believe that for at least one of you, I have something that will make your life what you've always thought it could be.

That's the purpose of this trip. That's the reason I took time to write this book. My goal has never been to change the world. It has never been to be known as a great speaker or writer. I believe it's much more focused than that.

Someday, after I'm gone, I believe that someone passing by will stop one of my children. Someone who will look them in the eye and tell them how their dad made a difference to them. When that happens, I'll know that my time here on this planet was well served. In my heart I'll know that while there were many days on this trip called life where we caught nothing, the ones we did hook went on to better things.

Fly-fishing is a sport. Fly-tying is an art. Fly-casting is a science. When you blend those absolutes together you end up with life as the final product. *Best of all, while participating in this great activity it is difficult to think about making a living. You tend to think about having a life.*

Come with me as I share my thoughts and my favorite fishing spots. As we spend this time together, let's not just talk. Let's spend time enjoying each other and also appreciating our own thoughts.

Life is not about how many you caught. It has more to do with how you react when you come home empty handed. Do you put your rod away forever or simply wait for another sunrise to do it all over again?

Life is taking in the water and everything around it. Appreciating the fact that you're there is far more important than if some fish takes your fly and runs with it.

"If you are unwilling to fail, you've already reached your maximum potential."

1

Getting Good Or Getting Going

It's May. Many of you are mowing lawns, cleaning pools, or getting the grill ready for a barbecue. Up in the Great North Woods of New Hampshire, the ice is just now thawing out of the lakes. Where the brush has provided shade, you can still crunch through some snow as you make your way toward the open water of the many streams.

For me, this was the time that I began to prepare for the season. I would inspect my rod for any damage, make sure that my reel was properly lubricated, and check out my supply of flies to see which needed replacing. And finally, I would begin to imagine what it would be like casting on my favorite spots.

It was also a time when I took my rod outside and began to practice. I'd gently snap my rod from the 10 o'clock position to the 2 o'clock until I was ready to lay it down on the water. I'd even find myself saying, "10 and 2. 10 and 2," over and over as I regained my rhythm that went stale over the winter months.

This year it was different. I had made a decision. Instead of staying on the lawn to get my rhythm down, I went up north to perfect my timing while in the water. What happened was a discovery that transcends the sport and translates to life. All the time I spent getting good, cost me fish I could have had if I'd only gotten going.

During the winter months when much of the water is frozen over, food is in very short supply. The fish instinctively slow down their metabolism almost to a dead stop. Their bodies become the same temperatures as the environment and they don't need very much food to keep going.

When the water begins to flow and the temperatures start to rise, the fish become extremely active. Since they have a temperature of near freezing, even a slight rise in water temperature "warms them up." That warmth shifts their metabolism into overdrive and they become ravenous feeders.

Trout are a species that have very good eyesight and they run at the slightest movement. That is why you almost need to sneak up on them when approaching the stream. The one exception is after the first thaw. Their hyperactivity and desire to feed throw caution to the wind. They eat constantly and are virtually fearless.

What that does for someone trying to get over his or her winter of inactivity regarding fly-fishing is create an atmosphere of forgiveness. Even poorly cast flies are often eaten as soon as they hit the water. This is one of those cases where you can improve as you go but you can also be rewarded for your efforts along the way. The reward may be as insignificant as a near miss from a curious trout. But it serves its purpose. It gives you just enough motivation to make one more cast.

That is the journey of success. If you look back at the life of someone you feel is successful, generally speaking, it isn't one event that took them to the top. Most times it is a series of steps, both forward and backward, that led to their destination. Experience shows that success is the willingness to always be ready to take just one more step.

While it is seldom one single event that makes someone successful, it's often just one experience that sets the tone. It's that one event that changes direction, emboldens commitment, or creates the ultimate motivation. As you look back over your life, perhaps you'll see such turning point events that happened to you. If you stick with this book, you'll see the life-long lessons that single experiences can teach.

People say that in life there are no guarantees. Many would say that rule applies to fishing as well. I disagree. Life and fishing for that matter have one guarantee that is universal. *If you are unwilling to fail, you've already reached your maximum potential.*

Taking Risks

Suppose you see a bend in a stream that has trout literally making the water boil as they slurp bugs from the surface. However, there are tree branches hanging over them that could tangle your line. You also notice that to the right of the action is a clear spot with no obstacles. It also has no fish. Where would you cast your line?

If you are afraid of losing your fly or tangling your line you might consider casting to the clearing. But, there are no fish there. While you could be assured of going home with your equipment intact, dinner would be awfully light. Or, you could risk it all and take the chance that maybe you could get just one cast to fall in the right spot.

In life, if you attempt nothing, you are guaranteed that result – nothing. Taking a risk however does not guarantee you'll succeed but it does create what makes life worth living. It creates possibility. Possibility is what keeps us in the game. It's what makes us try one more cast. When we focus on possibility there is no giving up.

Now, you could have kept throwing your line into the clear area and possibly the trout would shift their attention over there. But, looking at the activity under the branches, it isn't likely that your quarry is going to change its focus. So is it realistic to think they'll change course just because you offered something in a "safer" area? How possible is that?

Yet how many people continue along the same path hoping that the world will begin to see things their way and fortune will fall into their lap? How many people refuse to take a risk but curse the daily outcomes in their lives? They want success and happiness but only under ideal conditions.

Risking loss is the only way to open your life up to the possibility for success. Avoiding failure, or letting the fear of rejection take control, will hold anyone back from his or her true potential. If I wanted to enjoy a fresh fish dinner rather than settle for something out of a can and Rolaids®, I'd have to be willing to chance losing a fly or two.

Don't misunderstand me. I'm not suggesting that you simply heave your line directly at the branches and hope for the best. What I would expect is that you prepare for success while knowing that setbacks are a possibility. In this case, perhaps you would start with shorter casts so that the fly lands well in front of your target. Then with each successive cast, you get closer and closer.

Ultimately, the lesson learned is that the only possible way you have of succeeding in placing your fly directly in front of your quarry is to risk the possibility of a snag. Secondly, if your ultimate goal is to land your fish, snags along the way should not deter you from your final objective.

Whether it's a catch on a stream today or your life's dreams and ambitions, the same strong principles apply. You must be clear on exactly what you want to accomplish or where you want to end up. You must also have a strong desire showing why you want to accomplish this objective. Then you must use the best of your knowledge and abilities to move ever closer to your destination. Only then can you avoid the setbacks of self-doubt, fear of rejection and failure from causing you to end your quest.

There's an old saying that I attempt to live by when I'm seeking new levels in life. *If it's worth doing, it's worth doing poorly over and over until you get it right.* You cannot expect success at your first step any more than you should expect one setback from eliminating the possibility of achieving what you desire. It's a cumulative process of improvements, adjustments, and repetition. As in casting for a trout, it can take many casts to catch just one. And the more specific you are, the longer it may take. *Anything worthwhile requires effort until it's acquired.*

Too many people want instant greatness. They see or learn something new and expect to be an expert the first time they attempt it. When that doesn't happen, they tend to blame what they've learned instead of believing what they saw. They give up on their new technique or information because "they tried it once and it didn't work." What they should focus on is the success others have had using that same technique.

If people would stop treating new knowledge like instant pudding, they'd actually get to their goals faster. By not putting pressure on one's self to be an expert at something as soon as it is learned, one is given the opportunity to develop whatever is needed to become adept.

Worth The Effort

I saw a flash under what's commonly called a cutback in the stream. A cutback is where the water flow had worn away a piece of the bank and created a small overhang of bank which many times provide shelter to fish. I cast my line and let it drift toward the spot where I saw a bit of silver in the water. Sure enough, a beautiful trout made its way toward my fly. It was a trophy fish. However, just as I thought it would take the bait, it turned and went back in the shade. I had a choice to make.

I could have determined with one cast that the trout wasn't hungry today and I'd come back again at a more convenient time. Having seen the quarry and missed it, I could still share the story about how it got away. When offered advice by fellow anglers, I could boldly state, "I tried that, it didn't work." Even though I gave up, there would still be a risk. The risk is that this trophy would be caught by someone else before I could return. Or I could decide that what I really wanted was to catch this one fish and not pay attention to the results of any one attempt.

I repeated the process several times and each cast produced the same result. I changed flies several times and still the fish only came to take a look and go back home. During this ordeal, I also got my line tangled in the overhang on the bank and lost a few good flies. I was starting to get cold as the water flowing past my waders stole my body heat. But, that fish was a beauty. I decided to stay.

Cast after cast. Fly after fly. Nothing seemed to work. I was starting to get annoyed and discouraged. Evidently, so was my quarry. I tied on what I told myself would be the last fly of the day. I made my cast, kept my line from tangling, and let it drift into the cutback. Wham! Just like that it took the fly. Then, it took off.

The fish was heading downstream taking line. I had to follow as best I could with legs that had run out of strength from the cold water. Using every technique I had learned over the years, I began to turn it towards some shallow water where I'd be able to net the prize. As I got a good look at my adversary, the fact that it took nearly an hour and a half to hook it was lost in my mind. The battle was mine.

We both were growing tired and my thoughts were of getting the fish and then getting back to the cabin for a warm meal and shower. Those thoughts proved costly. As I got the fish exactly where I could reach it with a net, it turned onto its belly as if in surrender. Just as I was about to scoop it into the net, it gave one mighty twist, snapped the line and headed home.

I felt the twinge of failure. All of a sudden I began to question the folly of my efforts. The pain in my body magnified under the disappointment. I was nearly ready to give in at the beginning of my trip.

As we often do with any setback, I began to relive each step I took along the way. I became upset at how long I kept going after something that it was obvious I couldn't have. A twinge of anger set in as I counted each fly that was lost to branches, snapping wind knots, and snags. The cramps in my legs throbbed all the more as there was no prize for their efforts.

Then, I replayed the last cast. I saw my quarry rise and take the fly as it began to sink beneath the surface. As it retreated with what it thought was an easy meal, I set the hook by lifting my rod in the opposite direction. I think both of our hearts began pounding and our minds raced trying to think one step ahead of the other. I was breathing so heavily I think the leaves and branches moved. Man, what a great feeling.

I'd give anything to have that feeling again.

Then I realized all I had to do was risk losing a few more flies, suffering tight leg muscles, and getting so cold I almost couldn't walk. And after all of that, I knew that the outcome may not be any different. But, then again it might.

I think it would be worth it just for the feeling you can get from the chase. But imagine how you'd feel if the next time ended differently and your catch didn't get away. That possibility alone makes it worth taking one more shot. And therein lies the secret to life and happiness.

If you think about your own life I would imagine a flood of memories come to mind. If you focus on just one of them, others will come out of the storage cabinets of your conscious and subconscious. That tells you that your life, past, presents, and future is made up of a series of events and accomplishments. No single idea, action, or result has totally shaped you.

Life is not about the grand accomplishment. I believe the satisfaction comes from the willingness to just take one more shot. Instead of being overwhelmed by obstacles or setbacks that seem massive, think about real perspective. Think about taking just one more step.

Achieving any long-term goal is the result of effort and adjustment. Seldom does anything new work the first time. However, if you are committed to something worthwhile, and constantly make changes and shift your thought process after each attempt, over the course of time, you can expect to succeed.

"As is often the case, the difference between massive success and just being average is the willingness to expose yourself to risk."

2

Trailblazer Or Trailing

Safe Isn't Always Sound

In life as in angling, everyone has a favorite spot. That's the place where you feel comfortable and confident of the outcome. In fly-fishing, that's where you go when nothing is working and you really need to catch something. It's where you can cast your favorite fly and be fairly certain of the result.

For you it may be a drive to a certain place. Once you arrive you can put the day's distractions behind you and focus on ideas for improving a given situation. Or it may be a particular practice that brings things into focus so that solutions can be worked out.

But is it a place that only you know? Does the comfort you feel come from the knowledge that only you can find this place and participate in the feelings it brings? Or is it a place whose path is worn down by countless others who feel comfort in the familiar?

Are you merely comfortable because of familiar and popular surroundings? Can you find solutions in solitude or do you give up looking for the answer because you're looking for comfort?

One of the great joys my wife and I used to partake in was to get lost every weekend. Because we had recently moved to New England and didn't really know our way around, we would fill up the gas tank and drive. We had no destination or even specific direction in mind when we left. Since the kids weren't born yet, we had no specific time to be home. We just got lost – on purpose.

In getting lost we made discoveries. We discovered fantastic restaurants that we still visit today. Then we accidentally ended up at a lake or river clearing for a picnic. Entire towns with neat shops and places to see just seemed to pop up. Whatever we liked we noted on a map so we could come back. Whatever was uninteresting was forgotten. And all of these great discoveries happened by accident – on purpose.

Can You Fail Like Columbus?

I prefer to create new trails as many famous explorers have done before me. While I may not discover new lands, the simple joy of finding a new spot on a stream with the potential to produce the catch of the day is exciting. As I step where no one has before me, I think about the possibility of a fighting trout and not the rock that may cause me to stumble.

The essence of fly-fishing is a lot more than the microsecond it takes for your quarry to suck in the fly. It begins with the preparation and extends to the difficult hike to spots undiscovered. It continues with tangles created by gusts of wind and unforgiving branches that steal your hand tied flies. But every second of every mishap is masked by the ever-possible chance that the very next cast may produce the catch of a lifetime.

When Columbus did what earned him the right to take up countless chapters in our grade school history books, it was never really explained. When you peel away the layers of what actually occurred you are left with one startling fact - Columbus failed.

He never even came close to doing what he set out to do. In fact he couldn't have been further away from his planned destination if he stayed home. However, what made him into the historical hero he has become was not so much the discovery as it was the fact that he was willing to be the first to try.

Many great discoveries have been the result of failing at something else. However, it was the willingness to take the initial risk that really made things possible. If you look into an angler's fly case, their favorite is the easiest to spot. That's because there are a whole bunch of them. They know that while it is a dependable lure, they have to cast it into unpredictable situations and risk losing it to snags, overhangs and the like.

But, because they are risk takers to an extent, they have more than one in order to have every opportunity to succeed. There is an understanding that as long as one is willing to make at least one more cast regardless of the risk, there is an opportunity to catch a trophy fish. However, if one is only concerned with protecting flies and not willing to cast into risky waters, the odds of having "take-out" for dinner are greatly increased.

What Story Do You Tell?

How would you feel about a trip if this was the story you could tell?

"Well, you walk down this path to a wide open area. You throw your line into the water and wait. Sooner or later something will bite your fly and you reel it in. Then you go back to your cabin."

When you return home would you be excited about sharing your "adventure" with others? Do you see yourself planning to return to the same spot next year? Or, do you avoid opportunities to share your experience?

What would a trip like that be worth? In my opinion, even if you spent a dollar for the whole thing, you overspent. Trips like this are all about the events and sights, not just the outcome. Unless you're willing to risk mistakes, failing, lost gear, falls into a stream, or any other potential hazard, there is little chance of a memorable trip.

In many areas of the country there are ponds that are overstocked with trout or other fish. These places are about catching fish and nothing else. Experienced anglers may try new equipment or different flies just to see how they work. Learning how fish react to certain flies or presentations has value for future reference, but catching fish under these conditions is anything but exciting. Many times anglers take advantage of these situations as part of preparation for an upcoming trip.

When you face any challenge, look at it as if it were a fishing trip to an unknown area. Think of the potential as well as the risk. Then imagine being able to share the story, regardless of the outcome. *As is often the case, the difference between massive success and just being average is the willingness to expose yourself to risk.*

When taking the less traveled path, there are two possible outcomes. One, you will be able to warn others that this way leads to nothing and you can prove it with your experience. Or, you succeed in your quest because you were willing to risk facing the unknown.

In either case, you have something of value to pass along to others or use yourself. The point is, being confident has nothing to do with playing the safe bet all the time. While I'm not suggesting that you throw caution to the wind at every opportunity, I believe that *having a life as opposed to just making a living will involve taking risks.*

You can also succeed by following in the footsteps of others. That may sound contradictory but it really depends on who you follow. If you follow crowds, you end up not even knowing where you're going or why. But, if you find someone who is the type of success you'd like to be, there are many reasons to follow them step by step.

They are the leaders. The trailblazers. When you see yourself as an explorer, it's often best to follow those who have come before you, learn from the paths they chose, and then create some paths of your own.

The best leaders are nearly always the best servants. Initially, they would follow those they admired until their own confidence and commitment would take them on their own path to success. They would use the experience gained from watching others as a guide for their own success. But, when it comes time to choose, you must freely pick your own course.

"While I can't think of any preparation that would guarantee success, skipping steps or ignoring one altogether can almost certainly guarantee failure."

3

Loading The Line

No Slack In Success

Even those who are not fly fisherman admire the rhythm of the line as they bring the rod back and forth until just the right moment. Then they bring it forward one last time and lay it out on the water. Each subsequent cast is as poetic in motion as the last. But, careful preparation must be made between each or you risk a day of tangled disasters.

For the cast to be made, there must be a set motion that will be followed each and every time. There needs to be a right time to begin and end this motion, and most importantly, there must be absolutely no slack in the line. The elimination of this excess line, the removal of any slack is called loading the line. It is the final step prior to recasting your fly. It is also a critical step to make if you ever expect to hook your quarry.

This step is one of the more simple ones to execute. All that you need to do is strip the line in such a way as to take up any slack on the water. Take one finger from the hand holding the rod and hook the line through it. With the other hand simply pull the line through the finger until there is no slack between your rod tip and the fly in the water.

From that point forward, you are in total control of your rod, line, and fly. If you want to cast to a different area, you can. If you see a trout rising to take your fly, you're ready to set the hook. And, if the current creates more slack, you simply repeat the process.

The 90/10 Factor

In the business world, countless training budgets are exhausted on the closing of the deal. In sales, training is devoted toward closing techniques and signing contracts. It focuses on handling objections and moving toward the client's commitment. Yet, I believe that represents about 10% of the process.

Whether you're painting a room, going after a major account, or traveling to a spot where trophy fish have been known to be, preparation is critical to the payoff. Without preparing properly, you could be an expert sales closer, a top professional painter, or a world-class angler, and never get the results you want.

Don't get me wrong. Knowing exactly how to tell if a fish is taking your fly, how to set the hook, and when to let the fish run, are all very important to landing the prize. But step back a minute. Ask yourself some questions.

How successful would you be if you only took one fly on your trip? What would happen if your fishing reel jammed? What is the best line to use in a given situation? Where is the best place to locate fish? How long will it take to get there? What is the best time to be on the water?

The best fish I ever caught was also the one that gave me the most trouble reeling in. Even then, the entire process, from first cast to getting it in the net, took only an hour. And that included traveling about a half mile up stream to where the fish were feeding. The catch was a result of proper technique, good presentation, persistence, and a bit of luck. However, none of those elements were as important as preparing for the possibility.

Two weeks prior to the trip I began checking all of my equipment. I made sure that my waders didn't leak. I had my fly reel serviced and cleaned and replaced the line. My fly collection was restocked with all the ones I thought would be prevalent in the area I was heading.

Then I confirmed all of my reservations to make certain that I had places to sleep. I also checked to find out if the ice had indeed melted and that the rivers and streams were accessible. Finally, I left early enough to be able to get comfortable in my cabin and ensure a good night's sleep.

I did all that to make sure that my chances were good for that one hour of fishing that produced a nice catch. Some of you may think that's an awful lot of work for a trip that's supposed to be relaxing. Perhaps.

But, substitute my trip with any aspect in your life worth doing or having. Now imagine leaving out one or more element of preparation. What do you think it would do to your chances of success? The real question is, do you really want to find out?

Preparation is the key to things going as smoothly as possible when that moment of performance arrives. While boring as it happens, the resulting success makes it worthwhile. Preparation is also occurring right up until that very moment.

In addition to two weeks of preparation for my trip, everything leading up to and including that successful cast could be looked upon as preparation. Consider that very morning.

I ate a solid breakfast so that I could stay in the water longer without fatigue setting in. Fatigue can cause mistakes or make you rush certain parts of your technique, which would result in missing your target.

As I entered the stream area, I was careful to be cautious as I crept along the banks. While it certainly took longer to arrive at my final spot, I was able to enter the water unnoticed and I hadn't spooked any fish along the way. That meant I could slowly cast the entire area and cover any potential spots.

I began slowly turning over rocks to see what type of insect nymphs were there so I could determine what the fish were feeding on. This limited the amount of guesswork when it came to selecting the right flies to tie on.

And, even the right knot to use when tying on a fly is critical. The trout has a sensitive mouth and can feel any extra line hanging off the end of what you tied on. In addition, not using the right knot could mean a fish getting away because your knot didn't hold.

Other than the actual hiking along the stream, none of my other preparations took much time at all. Yet is there any one of them that you could choose to eliminate as a waste of time? Is there any step that could have been skipped without risking a day with no catches to show for your efforts?

Still, many of us in our daily lives continue to try and succeed without the necessary preparations to help improve the odds on success. *While I can't think of any preparation that would guarantee success, skipping steps or ignoring one altogether can almost certainly guarantee failure.*

One final note. As you bask in the glory of a well-prepared success, you should begin your preparation for your next event almost immediately. After a successful fishing trip but before I share my experiences with others, I begin preparing for the next outing. This is done by making sure all of my equipment is put away properly in its assigned place. I make notes of things that need repairs or adjustments and make plans to have them completed.

Now I can relax and tell my stories knowing that if someone wanted to leave first thing in the morning to do it again, I would be ready and prepared to go.

"Ultimately, the greatest risk reducing skill one can have is observation."

4

Fast Water Thinking

Still Waters Still Run Deep

Tranquil waters where the stream widens into a deep pool are usually very tempting. That is, provided you are there at the right time. You see the water is very clear and you can actually spot a lot of fish if you are careful in your approach. You also need to understand that if you can see them, they can probably see you.

Just downstream a bit is a spot where the water bends into a narrower path. There are a lot of rocks and the banks cut away providing shade. And, without getting into the laws of physics, the water is running faster. This is where you can increase your potential if you know how.

Trout love this type of water because it makes eating easier. Food just seems to be carried by and they can usually eat their fill without moving all that much. Anglers like it for much the same reason. They can cast into the flow and have their bait brought virtually to their quarry's mouth.

Because of the fast water, the sun can't get all the way through because of the ripples. The benefit to even a beginning angler is that the fish usually can't see you. That gives you an opportunity to get closer to where you want to cast and, in many cases, allows you to get clear of any obstructions.

Not As Easy As It Sounds

While it may seem as if the fish are more vulnerable in this situation, it's not always the case. Fast water presents a variety of challenges that can actually afford the fish more protection than in other areas.

Because of the speed of the water, anglers have to usually add weight to their lines to get the bait low enough to be eaten. That can, and often does, result in snags and hang-ups on the bottom of the stream. It becomes more important than ever to have total control over your line as it floats with the current.

The lack of visibility for anglers prevents you from knowing the actual depth in spots. While the speed of the water usually dictates that an area is shallow, you can come upon a hole deeper than you expected. These holes are usually discovered after you hook your quarry and are trying to land it.

The currents can also be the best friends a fish ever had. If they are hooked, they can head upstream and make you fight the current as well as their ability to run off with your line. Or they can go downstream and use the current to push them along and save their energy to fight a while longer.

Fast water thinking is anything but fast. It's rather detailed. As I used to tell my son as he was learning to drive, always have an out. That means plan for any eventuality and then have a back up prepared for your plan.

One assumption in fast water fishing is the catch. Hooking your quarry is one thing. Bringing it in for either a release or dinner is another. By assuming that you're going to get something to take your fly, you should have a target area where you can land your fish. That is usually a shallow spot or an area where the water is quieter.

You'll also need to focus on different paths in the event of a run. Should your catch take off in one direction or another, you need to know ahead of time how you'll follow. That prevents potential injuries and broken equipment due to falls from slipping or knocking into overhanging branches.

Life seems to always take place in fast water situations. It's therefore in your best interest to enter every situation with an out. In business, play the situation several ways. Instead of always thinking the worst, plan for the catch and run. Look for the successful agreement but be prepared for stipulations.

This type of life preparation comes across as if you are a quick thinker. It is really just being a professional and coming in prepared for any eventuality – even to the tiniest detail. By rehearsing situations you are always able to be proactive rather than reactive.

As with avoiding snags in fast water situations, when risking something new, control must be used. While there are unknowns in every new endeavor, you must strive to control those elements within your capabilities. In taking risks one doesn't leave everything to chance. Successful people eliminate as many unknowns as possible so that even the greatest risks are at a minimum.

When introducing your service or product to a new client, or letting old clients know about a massive change within your company, there are certainly risks involved. However, a professional will limit those risks to the things he or she can't control.

If it were a new product to be presented, one should be an expert at all the capabilities of that product. You should be well rested and prepared for the meeting, and dressed for the occasion. You should also get as much information about the company you're meeting with as possible so that you could demonstrate different applications of your product. In other words, you would limit the risk of how those seeing the presentation would react.

Even those reactions can be controlled to further limit risk. As you do enough presentations, you will begin to see common reactions. That's why successful sales people become even better over time. They are constantly adjusting based on their face-to-face experience.

Ultimately, the greatest risk reducing skill one can have is observation. In fast water situations, looking at the surroundings and keying in on subtle changes can make all the difference in the day. The same goes for business. Being able to adjust to suit the needs of a client or coworker may mean the difference between a successful meeting and a lost cause.

Watching as a trout repeatedly rises to eat can reveal a pattern. Someone who is not very observant will often cast to the last rise. The patient angler looks for the pattern and casts to where they believe the trout will rise next. Had their observations taken into account what the fish was feeding on and then matching that source with the right fly, success will look easy.

Simple? Perhaps. Easy? Not ever. The simplicity is knowing that one must be observant. Simply watch for all of the telltale signs and act accordingly. That skill is acquired over time and through many failings of missed opportunities. Also, the willingness to make the necessary adjustments to improve one's chances must be present.

Too many want the easy answers. These people are quick to find fault in everything but the right thing. You can identify their lack of habit and consistency in nearly everything they do. Every time something doesn't work, they throw it all away and reinvent the wheel. They would save so much more time and achieve greater success if they would adjust rather than destroy.

Success is nothing more than a series of adjustments and building upon what you've learned. However, you must make the changes and build upon your experience as well as on the experience of others. If someone who has fished a particular stream all their lives tells you that there are no fish below the dam, why would you spend valuable vacation time trying to prove them wrong?

It All Adds Up

Success is always a compilation. It's made up of adjustments, new information, observations, and experience. Focus and flexibility are important elements of the equation and are skills that improve with time and repeated use.

Just as it is being on a swift running stream, you must focus on the areas where the fish will most likely be. But, you can't stop there. Now you must look for areas where you can safely cast and then for areas where you can lead your catch so that you can successfully land it.

If all of these elements aren't present, you must be flexible enough to move to an area that better suits your objective. You can't be in a spot that doesn't allow a way out if you land a fish and it runs up stream. You also can't derive much enjoyment from a place that's perfectly safe in every aspect, but has no potential for catching fish.

You must put limits on either side of your considerations. You can't make yourself so safe that you are away from any fish any more than you should head towards a feeding frenzy where you'll most likely be swept away by the current. You need to minimize risk while maximizing the potential for success.

In business that means you must avoid being too careful. Trying to make the perfect presentation to the perfect prospect under perfect conditions will never happen. That is, unless, you expose yourself to every possibility. In other words, if you really know what you want to say, and are willing to say it to anyone who will listen, you could very well run into the perfect client.

However, you also need to refine your presentation or demonstration based on observations. These adjustments make you better each time and ultimately lead to a higher rate of success. You can't just practice; you need to be more active.

You must be as prepared as possible, but at the same time you should also be willing to fail. This is where you can learn and adjust. But adjusting is different than trying something totally different each time you meet a new client or prospect.

Just as you would expect to catch something when you tie on your favorite fly, you have to be willing to change it if nothing is biting it. But, before you change flies, maybe you change the way you cast. Perhaps you try a different retrieve. Or, you even let your line drift to an entirely different spot. Basically, you exhaust all possibilities before making a change.

Just as in business, the changes shouldn't be massive in most cases. It's often a minor adjustment that makes all the difference. If you were trying to get a company to buy nuts and bolts from you and were arguing over price, you wouldn't suddenly try selling nails, would you? While that may seem like an over simplification, check the rest of your practices. Have you ever found yourself saying, "I tried that once, it doesn't work."

It's often a minor and sometimes unnoticed adjustment that makes all the difference. If you start with minor changes and work your way toward the possibility of making a major concession instead of the other way around, you'll arrive at a satisfactory solution in the least expensive and most timely fashion.

"People hate to be sold – but they love to buy!"

5

Rises, Ripples, And Reward

The main sources of food for trout are different insects living near the water. Many of them are actually born in the river, stream, or lakes that are also inhabited by the fish. Those who begin life in the water often get eaten at different stages of development.

Eggs are deposited in the water to hatch. When they do, what arrives looks nothing like the insect it will become. At this cycle in life they are referred to as nymphs. Early in the season, trout gorge themselves on the abundance of nymphs that are often just floating with the current.

At a certain point of development, these nymphs become ready to shed their skin and become the flying insects they were meant to be. The amazing sight is when they actually shed their skin right on the surface of the water, stretch their wings and fly off. Maybe.

Trout can rise to the surface and take these insects right into their mouths. This occurrence is often called the hatch even though these insects have left their egg behind long ago. But, on bright sunny days it can seem as if the water is boiling as trout lose their cautious nature for a buffet that seems endless.

While it may look easier to land your fish on days like this, you still need to select the right fly and present it without spooking the fish. This is when you need to control your excitement and put a little thought into your selection.

Talking Your Way Past Success

The same thing can happen in business. You seem to hit upon the right situation. The prospect is starting to feel the enthusiasm right along with you. The next thing you know, every excuse in the book is being used to put you off, "…let me think about it"; or, "…call me in a week."

Sensing excitement isn't all that difficult. Keeping quiet, while waiting for their reaction, sometimes feels impossible. But, that's exactly what you need to do. The prospect is concentrating on feeding their excitement and often with what you've shared so far. Don't break their excitement or frighten them away just because you weren't finished with what you wanted to say.

In business there is an expression that you should keep in mind. *"People hate to be sold – but they love to buy!"* Let your people buy. Give them the information that they've asked for and wait for a reaction. Don't be concerned with sharing all of your knowledge regarding what you have to offer. No one buys because of what someone knows. People buy for themselves.

Let them buy. You'll still get credit for the sale. No one ever achieved massive success by simply talking. However, I know many who have become multi-millionaires because of their ability to really listen. Taking the time to really hear what a potential client, prospect or associate is saying may give you information that will later help in arriving at a mutually agreeable success. I've always trained people to believe that everyone you meet with will tell you everything you need to know in order to arrive at a positive decision. What prevents that from happening is your unwillingness to let them speak.

All Knowing or All Caring

When I came around the bend in the stream, there was a calm section that was just filled with ripples and rising trout. I could have run up to the bank, jumped into the water and started casting. But I didn't. Even though I could see the volumes of fish and knew that they were feeding on what looked like exactly what I had tied onto my line, I didn't rush.

Slowly and low I crept up to the weed line on the bank. I pulled some line off the reel and began to move my rod into a casting rhythm. Gently, I laid the line on the surface with my fly touching down without much disturbance. Then I waited. I twitched the line to create the look of fluttering wings on the water and then it happened. Just a slight rise and my fly was quietly slurped into the mouth of a waiting brown trout.

Even as I led this trout to the banks of the stream where I could use my net to finalize the catch, I never stood up. No shouts of joy or speedy retrieve as I won this battle. I didn't want to oversell this catch. Why not?

From the crouched position I had taken and the slow retrieval, it was difficult to know exactly how big or small this catch really was. If it was small and I had jumped with excitement, it was likely that any other fish in the area would have been spooked and then the one I had hooked would represent the end of the line for the day.

Any experienced angler would know that. However, only an angler who cared enough about the possibility of others using these waters would follow this practice. I knew that if this catch were big enough, I'd be done for the day or go looking for another place to try. That being the case, I didn't want to ruin this great spot for anyone else who was hiking in that day.

It's like that in the rest of one's life. How you react to minor successes often determines your opportunity at even greater ones. Some have a tendency to over celebrate little accomplishments and they often desire all the credit. Unfortunately, that usually results in a lack of support when a major challenge comes up.

The Rewards

When searching for a trout in a stream, your objective is to get them to put something in their mouth that isn't good for them. You want them to take your bait. But with plenty of food around them, they aren't going to do work extra just because you've got a good-looking fly.

All of the elements necessary for success must be in place. Having patience, remaining still, staying calm as you watch the fish come toward your fly, are all part of the process. But so is having a good knot to hold your fly in place, or patching any leaks in your waders before you leave home to keep the cold water from cramping your legs.

It's doing the obvious while also preparing in advance. It's Leaving yourself with the answer to the question, "What if I catch one?" and looking at your situation to find all of the options.

Most people prepare for an eventual failing. Consequently, they're often ready for just that. Seldom do you hear planners ask what would happen if their idea were massively successful. Yet, without planning for the possibility of success, aren't we limiting the true potential?

While I am all for preparing for the possibility of things not going according to plan, I also feel very strongly about planning what might happen if everything goes right. However, I wasn't always this way. Most of my planning went for protecting against failing. This story may help.

The $54 Trout

When my son was very young, he wanted to learn to fish. One Christmas, he got a rod and reel as a present and couldn't wait to use it. Up here in the Northeast, that's difficult to do in the winter. As soon as April arrived, he couldn't wait anymore. I finally agreed to take him fishing.

April up here is still quite cool. In fact, on this particular day the wind and the temperature made it impossible to fish on any of my traditionally favorite spots. And, as my son was still learning about fishing, it was important that he catch something, otherwise he'd lose interest.

I suddenly remembered a place that was heavily stocked and you actually paid for the fish you caught. Even though that doesn't sound all that sporting, I was more interested in having something on the end of my son's line.

As we checked in, I noticed the sign. Small fish $.25 per inch. Large fish $9.00 per pound. Being prepared for failing, I assumed that we'd catch a couple of small trout, spend a few dollars and go home. Everybody would be happy. When the owner warned my son about the "big" ones and then looked at me, I thought he was just playing for my son's sake.

When we got to the edge of the water, I tied a hook on my son's line, put some bait on and handed him the rod. I figured that I'd let him cast a bit until I got my equipment ready. Wrong.

His line no sooner hit the water than it began heading across the pond. Instinctively he lifted the rod and set the hook. "I got one Dad!" he screamed, "Get the net." He insisted on bringing in this one all by himself and, between the strain and the smiles, that's just what he did.

As I got it in the net, I guessed its size. One pound. We had been fishing less than three minutes and I'm $9.00 in the hole. Of course, with the look of satisfaction on my son's face, I knew we couldn't leave.

Luckily, he thought that it would be this easy every time. After I put more bait on his line he kept casting and retrieving too fast for any fish to bite. In the meantime, I got my equipment ready to fish.

It was great watching as he became better with each cast. Finally, I told him to slow down a little and see what happens. He cast out as far as he could, and then waited. Unfortunately, not for long. He had another one. As he reeled this one in, I was relieved to see that it was much smaller than the first, so we'd only be paying for inches. Ten inch fish - $2.50.

He looked at me and said that now it was my turn. He wanted me to catch one as well. This was the first time in my life I wasn't hoping for the big one of the day. Luck was with me. As I cast out and retrieved, nothing was being aggressive enough to take my lure. And my son was getting tired of waiting. He cast his line out, put his rod down and began exploring the bank for frogs.

Just then, I felt a hit on the end of my line. Lifting the rod tip, I set the hook and breathed a sigh of relief. I had a fish, and it wasn't very big. My son came running over to help with the net. As he scooped the trout he looked back at me and said, "At least you caught one, Dad."

Another ten-inch trout.

I figured after $14.00 it was time to go. As my son and I began gathering all of our stuff, I noticed something out of the corner of my eye. His rod was heading into the water. Before I could say anything, he was on it. He grabbed the rod and as he lifted it, the tip stayed down.

You could see the line peel off the reel as well as the strain on my son's face. Yet he insisted that he could do this all by himself. While part of me really wanted this monster to snap the line, I couldn't disappoint my son. I began giving him instructions to land his fish.

As I stood ready with the net, I could see the silver flash of this trout as it tried to turn and run. My son was as patient as a saint and did everything right. Finally, it was in the net. It was as fat as a football and nearly two feet long. It weighed six pounds. Reaching into my pocket I knew that the $25.00 I had wasn't going to be enough.

It was the first time in my fishing experience where the most important piece of equipment was a credit card. That fish alone was $54.00 and the total bill was $68.00.

Imagine your business or job with that kind of planning. Being prepared to handle success is just as critical as having a backup plan in the event something goes wrong with your initial idea.

That's why, when I'm prepared on the stream, I can relax and enjoy the moment. Nothing is going to create distractions or tension because of a surprise. If a giant trout takes my fly and runs upstream, I have a plan. If nothing bites my favorite lure, I have a plan. And at this point in my life, so that I can spend more time in places like this – I HAVE A PLAN.

"*Failing is a great teacher and making adjustments to failing is the fastest way to success.*"

6

Tying One On

It Really Is The Little Things

While there are rods that cost thousands of dollars and matching reels that approach that same price level, I'm not in that league. But, fly-fishing isn't the least expensive sport to participate in. Set-ups even for amateurs like me range from a few hundred to over a thousand dollars. Let's split it down the middle and say a complete rod, and reel outfit can cost $500.

Now add to that the cost of waders, specific types of fly line, an assortment of flies, a net, fly vest, and of course, the trip and you have a sizable investment. However, it does give a lot of pleasure both in the moment and for years of memories. If you enjoy something, it's worth it.

But, it all comes down to the smallest detail as to whether or not you ever have any memories to think about. Even if you bought the top of the line equipment, found the best places to fish, and tied on the perfect fly for the situation, you may never even come close to catching anything. Unless you know which knot to tie.

Something as simple as a knot can be the difference between a great experience on the water and a disappointment that can ruin the entire trip. While you are certain to lose flies from low hanging branches or snags in the water, or have fish come off as you try and hook them, losing one because your line unties is just inexcusable.

There are enough hazards on the water without inventing one. While this book encourages risk, I hope it also shares how to prepare so that certain obstacles can be avoided. Although you would think that tying the correct knot would be second nature, how many times have you prepared for the big things only to have something small and basic ruin the event?

In many of my training programs, I encourage failing. I want people to not only fail, but fail fast. *Failing is a great teacher and making adjustments to failing is the fastest way to success.* Plus, getting through one failing and making another attempt gives you confidence. However, encouraging one to fail does not give them license to be careless, lazy, and haphazard in their approach. You can't go into a new

Tying One On

situation with inadequate and outdated information. Quite the contrary.

You need to be as prepared as is humanly possible. If it's a business situation that we're discussing, you should have all of your bases covered to the best of your ability. You should know your product or service and its benefits inside out. The bottom line is, you should be totally prepared to succeed. But if you do fail, you must make the adjustments, put the same effort in preparing again and then hit the field, ready to play.

It's like having a full toolbox. You can own every tool imaginable and know how to use each and every one. But, you also know that most jobs will only require certain tools. Even though you won't use every tool on every job, you can find comfort in knowing that they are there in case you need them.

It's the same thing with knowing your job, opportunity, or products. You should never need all of the information about every aspect, but you should feel confidant and comfortable knowing that you can.

You're Reading A Perfect Example

Hopefully you're gaining value and enjoyment from this book. But, I want you to understand, this isn't what I originally wrote. The entire book has been through an evaluation process, editing, and a collection of corrections and suggestions. This insures that you get the most benefit from my ideas.

Yet, when I finished the first draft, I can honestly say, it was my best effort. I was totally prepared to write. I dedicated specific times to sit and focus on the subject matter. And upon completing the manuscript, I sent it in. I was prepared to succeed.

Then came the other eyes. Those who read it had their own ideas of what to expect. Their expectations were either met or not and from there we adjusted. I would take their suggestions as well as necessary corrections, and make another pass. This time it went more quickly than the original writing. And as we continued to work together, my writing improved and the editing became less frequent.

If you stop the process, I would have failed. I could have failed sooner if I had let my ego make the demands that what I wrote the first time is as good as it gets. Fortunately, my goal is to end up with a book that has impact with the readers at a high level of quality. To achieve that in any endeavor requires that egos remain locked up and that you have an open mind.

The point is, I was as prepared as I could have possibly been. As a writer, I write. While that may sound like an over simplification, it means I have done everything possible to create the mental and physical atmosphere that is suited to good writing. That means right down to a comfortable chair.

Even the smallest distraction can ruin your train of thought. That may mean a lost trophy trout because of a poorly tied knot, or a wasted day of writing for the sake of a chair that constantly needed adjusting.

Looking At It Another Way

Nothing succeeds like simplicity. It's the simple things we think, do or say that often produce great results. On the water, simple may mean finding a way to get closer to the action without being seen.

If the area you need to cross is wide open, that may seem like an impossible task. But, you aren't thinking simply. It really isn't important that *you* get closer to the action. What really matters is that your *fly* gets closer. Figuring out how to make that happen becomes the challenge.

Just when you're about to give up after many casts trying to sail your line farther than ever before, it hits you. Since you're on a stream, let out enough line so it can eventually float to where you want it to be. What could be simpler?

Those of you who have never lived the frustrations of fishing with a fly rod must be thinking that the above solution smacks of the obvious. And it does. In fact, the person who made that suggestion to me had never thrown a fly before. There are times when you need not only a different set of eyes but also a different thought pattern to come up with the right answer. And, as long as your ego can stand it, you have a better chance of landing the big one.

Answers are all around us but sometimes we only look in the standard places. In sales, the latest sales manual may not have what you're looking for but the way a total stranger handles a situation may be the answer. I can't tell you how many business lessons I've learned over the years just by watching children. Their innocence often gets right to the heart of a situation without complicating things. Isn't that how business should run?

Experience is a great teacher but nothing says that it always has to be *your* experience. When building a business it is always wise to follow the paths created by those who came before you. Especially if they've achieved a level of success that is where you want to end up. But, never let yourself be limited by what others have accomplished. Remember, before they succeeded, whatever was being used was the best way to get things done. They came along, improved it or simplified it, and achieved success.

Letting other people's experience serve you is a great way to accelerate success. Why would you repeat mistakes that have already been made when there are others who will share their information with you – just for asking.

"If someone has drawn a map to a destination you'd like to visit, why not follow it?"

7

Getting Guidance
From A Guide

Spending More Avoids Waste

In different parts of the country, and even in different types of water, trout act and react differently. In deep pools they may not rise to the surface as often as they do in shallow flowing streams. In lakes they may even stay deep year round. How they react near rocky bottoms as opposed to sandy or muddy areas can be dramatically different. So you need to be ready for anything.

But, you've waited all year for this trip. Scrimped, saved, worked extra for the time off – you name it, you did it. Now that you're there, why risk everything on ignorance and inexperience. You need to decide if it's worth spending a little more to hire an experienced guide to get you to the fish or risk everything you've spent on a chance that you may get lucky.

That's one way of looking at it. The other way is to focus on enjoying every aspect of the trip regardless of the in-stream results. You can take in all of your surroundings, enjoy the fresh air, and feel the anticipation that the possibility of hooking a trophy catch creates.

But what if you want to experience the thrill of the catch? Suppose your entire purpose of taking a trip to a new area is to find out if everything you've heard is true? You've got to do something to increase your odds. You hire a guide: Someone who has experience on the water you want to explore. A person who knows what to tie on the end of your line. And an expert who can make you better than when you arrived. Whatever the price for someone like that, it has to be worth it compared to going home after wasting money on a miserable trip – especially if you could have avoided the misery.

In the outdoors, a guide serves multiple purposes. Their knowledge of the area gets you to the right spot for the best chance of success. Then they help with coaching as you cast your fly to the areas their experience has taught them the fish are located. And finally, they take you step by step as you try and land the fish you've caught. Basically you're using someone's experience to help you achieve success. *If some-*

one has drawn a map to a destination you'd like to visit, why not follow it?

That is also the fastest way to succeed in business. Experience is the best teacher is an old expression. However, there is no rule that says all the experience must be yours or even experienced first hand. You can learn a tremendous amount from those who blazed the trail before you. These people achieved success by taking a path that they created. Now you can follow their lead and avoid some of the pitfalls and setbacks they suffered on their journey.

Being Successful and Being First Have Nothing In Common

Many people have achieved their life's dream by listening to the guidance of others who went before them. They saw a level of success that was attractive and followed the steps of those who went before. Offered information was gladly accepted as was instructions on potential pitfalls.

While there are those who have achieved success by "discovering" something, there are countless more who have incredible lives because they followed someone as successful as they wanted to be.

Learning from the experience of others is only valuable if you act upon your new knowledge. Because you have to do the work for yourself, your success is not diminished because you weren't the first to achieve it. For example, suppose you wanted to become a millionaire. If you followed the direction and guidance of someone who had achieved that goal and you succeeded, your millionaire status would be just as valid as theirs.

You can also use other people's experience to develop new directions in your business or your life. You can see results from particular actions and predict how similar actions will create results in your new endeavor.

On the stream you watch as your guides cast a dry fly. They let it sit on top of the water for just a moment. Then they skillfully twitch their line to make it look like a real insect fluttering on the surface of the water. That twitching sends out a vibration that may attract a fish looking for a meal. In other words, the fly is made to look as real as possible.

Now, you're in a different spot, perhaps a deep pool along the stream. After watching, you notice that nothing is rising. You know there are fish in the area and you decide to change flies to go after them. You use a type of fly called a streamer. This fly is made to be under water and is designed to look like a small fish. Your past experience tells you that looks aren't everything. You remember your guide moving the line to make it look more realistic. Using that experience, instead of twitching the line you pull it toward you to mimic the swimming motion of a real fish.

Guiding Others For Your Success

One of the questions I often ask in business seminars is this, "Are you training your replacement?"

Regardless of what is really happening in the organization, the answer is always yes. If you do nothing with people under your care and supervision, the company will never have a replacement for you so that you can be promoted. You become "too valuable" on that level.

However, if you are willing to constantly work toward improving those under your responsibility, you will receive two very distinct benefits. Not only will you earn the respect of those who look to you for leadership but you will also improve your own performance.

I was able to witness that with my son. He is a pitcher with the goal of being selected to play in college on a scholarship. He was having trouble with some of his pitches and couldn't quite figure out what he was doing wrong. You could see the stress mounting and I wanted to take his mind off the situation.

A good friend of mine was coaching a team of 10 and 11 year olds. I asked if he could use some help with his pitchers and offered my son as a coach for a day. He gladly accepted and my son and I went to practice.

As a teenager my son was on top of the world to have an audience hanging on his every word. First of all, he's 6'4", which makes him a giant among the kids. He lined them all up and began showing them how to loosen up and stretch to prevent injury. Then, one by one he shared the proper motion and mechanics to control the location and speed of the pitches. Over and over he demonstrated the proper techniques until they were able to duplicate his efforts. It was a fun day to watch, as my son was the center of attention because he was teaching others what had made him a better athlete.

I could stop there and this would be a great story. But, it actually gets better. At his next game, my son was virtually unhittable. His control of the baseball was better than ever, and he showed no signs of strain as he threw late into the game. Every move he made was perfect.

At practice, he couldn't seem to concentrate on any aspect of what he was doing. He was looking everywhere for a solution to a problem that was literally right in front of him. But, by actually not thinking about himself, and sharing for the benefit of others, he improved his skills and took his game to a new level.

"If you master the process, the results will always take care of themselves."

8

That's Why They Don't Call It Catchin'

Wisdom Of The Ages

As I slowly approached my truck, an old timer was heading for the stream. When I nodded hello, I could tell he noticed my empty stringer. I'm sure he also noticed that the look on my face was not the look of someone who wanted to discuss the pleasures of catching the river's best.

He grinned and looked me in the eye as he said, "That's why they call it fishin'." I must have looked like he was speaking another language because he took a step closer, pointed to my empty net and

added very matter-of-factly, "If the results were supposed to be different, they'd call it catchin."

While it's hard to translate his north woods
accent into the written word, just the way it sounded
made me laugh. He was being good-natured about it
and I'm certain I'm not the only one to ever leave the
stream empty for the day. But, upon recollection, it
may have been one of the most valuable lessons I've
ever learned.

Success Is The Process Not The Result

Did you ever see an ad in the paper looking for
sales people? "WANTED-TOP CLOSERS," or something to that effect. Closing the deal is when the
client/customer says yes. They wanted to hire people
who could get other people to say yes. Simple, right?
Not very smart though.

If closing the deal, or finishing the job were all it
took, we'd all be rich. Anyone can learn to close
deals. But, those who are successful in sales, or any
other aspect of business or even life understand, it's
not about results. It's about the process. *If you master the process, the results will always take care of themselves.*

If you're willing to get out on the water day after
day and learn the different techniques of casting for
different conditions, you'll get results. If you try different fly patterns in different colors and use them in
different ways, the results will happen. If you're willing to hike into the woods a little further, turn over a

few more rocks to see what the food source is, be willing to stand in colder water, you'll get what you're after.

That old timer taught me well. I don't care how many goal setting seminars and motivational talks you've heard. It doesn't matter how much positive thinking you do or how committed to achieving your objective you are. You can't start at the result!

You'll never be able to walk up to a total stranger and have the first words out of your mouth be, "So, do we have a deal?" Not unless you're looking for a definite "no."

In life, and in business, and even in fishing, you take all of your knowledge and experience and file it for use as you approach the right time. But, if you're not willing to go through the process, you can't expect to get your end result.

A Simple Success Secret

Achieving success in any area of life or business is a continuing process of effort and adjustment preceded by proper preparation. We prepare as best we can, given the information and experience we have over a particular situation, then we execute.

If we don't achieve the desired results we either abandon or adjust. If you can take the experience and knowledge from a setback and make adjustments to your plan of action, by process of elimination you should come up with a winning combination.

How long will that take? That's a common question. However, the real question is, are you willing to fail fast? If you are, you can speed through the process until you develop the right combination.

Avoiding The Mourning Process

You're new. As part of your initial training you learn that the first thing you need to do is set up an appointment. Once you have the appointment, you deliver your information and ask for a decision. Simple.

You did it. Someone said yes to a meeting with you. You're so excited you almost want to throw a party to celebrate. Containing your enthusiasm is nearly impossible and you become totally focused on this meeting. Then the date arrives.

You meet. You explain. You get turned down. The pain you feel is like nothing you've ever felt before. It seems reasonable that you go through a period of mourning and maybe even some therapy. You tell yourself that it will be a long time before you put yourself through that again.

What will you accomplish that way? Very little, I suspect. If success comes from meeting people and explaining your offering, how will you ever succeed? That's why you need to fail fast – and often. Especially in the beginning.

Let's start again. Only this time you're so excited about setting an appointment that you go ahead and set another, and another.

You get to your first meeting and the results are just like the one above. No good. You feel bad. You're just about to go into mourning but then you realize that you have another meeting for which to get ready. As you head out to that meeting, you evaluate what you did at the first one, make adjustments, and actually start feeling confident again. You meet. Same results.

Now you really start to feel bad. You're sure that a pity party would be okay right about now and then you realize, you have another meeting.

Even if the results are the same, you've learned valuable lessons. Their answers are not going to determine your career decision. You can continue setting appointments and developing techniques while gathering experience. And, when you do succeed, you'll be in the habit of simply setting up more meetings. Ultimately, you will have a presentation that is yours alone. Then when people turn you down, you can be confident that it wasn't your presentation; it may have been something beyond your control.

On the water, the technique would be fan casting. This is merely casting repeatedly moving your line across an area, a little at a time. Then, you change flies and repeat the process. You can also alternate the way you retrieve each fly to determine not only which fly will work but also which presentation is most effective.

Each cast that doesn't produce a fish is a failing. Yet it does provide some information. It's those who are willing to accumulate information that find it easier to control their destiny. They are the ones who understand the difference between failing and failure.

Failing is merely the event. Casting to no result would be a failing, as would losing one of your flies to an overhanging branch.

Failure is when the event takes control. For example, if you were heading out to a fishing spot that you had heard about, and planned for weeks to get there, would you make one cast, catch nothing, and go home? That would be a failure.

You're probably thinking about how ridiculous that would be. No one would go to all that trouble, make one attempt and give up. Would they? Unfortunately, it happens all the time.

The next time you hear of an idea at a presentation, listen to the response. Have you ever heard someone say, "We tried that once; it didn't work." In business this is often the cause of prolonged failing. People of this mindset often spend time reinventing the wheel. Every idea gets one shot to work. If it doesn't, it's out.

What if you were to try fan casting at your job, or business, or even in your life? You quickly cover the possibilities, note the results, make changes, and do it all over. You'll find that eliminating minor points and setbacks will often result in the perfect solution. And, isn't that what you're after?

No, No, 100 Times No!

When I'm presenting a bit about my background, I often share the story of how I was turned down by over 100 publishers before I signed my first book contract. As you may imagine, I'm often asked how I was able to keep going in spite of all that rejection.

While I'd love to give you a profound answer, there isn't one. In fact, I caution you not to feel insulted by the simplicity of the truth. The fact is, I never knew how many times I was turned down until after I signed my first contract. I just never counted the "no's."

In hindsight, the reason I kept sending out letters was because of my focus. I was intent on seeing my name on the cover of a book. The legal side of being published is the fact that you can only sign a contract with one publisher per book. Understanding this let me believe that the negative responses weren't all that important because I only needed one to say "yes."

While I did make adjustments to my proposals along the way, I still never really spent time thinking about each rejection. Had I analyzed each one and focused on every negative response, it's likely that I never would have even finished my first book, let alone do eight more.

The answers along the way aren't important until you hear the one that gets you to your desired destination. The secret is the willingness to keep exposing yourself to potential answers. The only ones you need to focus on are the ones that are important to you and your quest.

Imagine being out on the stream and making your first cast. Everything goes well and the fly settles on the water without a ripple. Then…nothing. No rise, no near miss, just nothing. Now what? Do you throw away your rod? Head for home? Tell the world that fly-fishing never works? Of course not. You're there to fish. One cast can't determine the entire trip. Or can it?

The cast that catches *the* fish of the trip is one you'll remember in great detail. When the elusive trout takes your fly and then takes off, everything inside you speeds up. Your heart, your breathing, and everything else are moving at hyper speed. Yet, doesn't your mind see everything in slow motion?

When someone who has experienced that is asked to describe the event, they can do it with vivid detail. But, I'll bet if you asked them how many casts it took to achieve success, they couldn't tell you. That's because it's not important. What's important is that they believed in themselves and had a goal of catching a fish. They knew that the only way to fail was to quit and go home.

Why can't we do that in business and in life? Much of the time we spend giving up could be better used focusing on where we want to be rather than what just occurred. Instead of going for it again, we give up and go home and then tell ourselves why it wasn't meant to happen. We tell ourselves whose fault it really was. We tell ourselves that we'll never put ourselves in that situation again.

Now, I love fly-fishing but it will never become more important to me than my life goals. That being said, why would we be so persistent casting over and over until we catch a fish, and yet we give up on a life changing opportunity after just one attempt?

"Those who dream have the courage to take one more step, make one more attempt, and end up closer to their goals."

9

Small Brains, One Focus

Even Dead Fish Can Follow The Current

Catching trout in a stream is always more of a fight than in lakes or ponds. The reason is that swimming against a constantly moving current makes those in the stream stronger. Not only are the fish trying to catch food that is moving at the speed of the current, they do it without changing location. Their bodies are almost entirely muscle as pushing against the resistance of the current has strengthened them.

That's the entire capability of these fish: eating and getting stronger. The larger ones are those that do it better and longer than their peers. Those who can't at the least maintain in the current don't survive. They may be washed down stream into the mouths of predators. It's possible that they end up in an area not rich in food and die. Those who survive are constantly battling to stay up stream and go against the current.

In business there is a rule called the 80/20 rule. Simply stated the rule says that 80% of the money is earned by 20% of the team. 80% of business is closed by 20% of the staff. 80% of goals are achieved by 20% of the workers. And so on.

This rule is probably as old as business. But, even though everyone knows of this rule, the majority still spends time trying to fit in with the masses who just get by. They generally are more worried about what others think about them than they are about getting to their goals. They allow the thoughts and opinions of others dictate their future.

It's easy to go with the current. In fact, it takes very little effort to fit in. Success comes from swimming up stream or going against the grain. How often have we heard the expression, "If it's so good why isn't everyone doing it?" Many times the real answer is, "I don't know."

Maybe it is so good *because* not everyone is doing it.

Focus Pocus
We know that fish have very small brains and only act instinctively. They can only focus on what's

right in front of them and what will help them survive. Fortunately, we are more sophisticated than they are in that we have the ability to create thought and focus on our desired outcomes. Our lives are shaped by how well we use that gift.

On the water you focus on where you want the fly to land. You can't have your eyes wandering over the scenery and watching your line as you bring the rod up and then snap it forward. Doing that will leave the landing to random chance, rather than near your desired location.

In life, focus plays the same role. If we continue to see where we want to end up rather than be distracted by events and results along the way, it's likely we will arrive near our chosen destination. *Having focus isn't magic but the results from being focused can be magical.*

Here's some help for getting focused.

Find and build relations. Make it a goal to meet someone new every day. That doesn't mean you need to do business with them or even discuss what you do. Just meet them and listen to their story. Perhaps you have something that might be helpful to them in their life or work. Or, they may be able to offer you some help and guidance in yours.

Open yourself up to possibilities not perceptions. Ask yourself this question, "What's that got to do with my dreams?" *Those who dream have the courage to take one more step, make one more attempt, and end* *up closer to their goals.* Those who don't will often justify where they are in life and make it sound okay.

Construct a database. That's high-tech for make a list. If you meet people every day, your list will never end. Each person on your list can be someone you'd like to know better, someone who can use what you have to offer, or someone who has the very experience to help you.

Use leverage. Be unique in the way you meet people. Create memories rather than walls. Focus on being approachable. Always leave people the opportunity to return for another chance if something changes in their lives. When you have a strong relationship with someone, that person will help you achieve your goals. That means you'll get there faster.

Stop wanting to. Instead, have to. Many people want to accomplish things. Nothing happens because you want it. Years ago, I *wanted* to write a book. Nothing happened. But because I had dug a hole so deep that the only way out was to sell a lot of copies of a book, I *had* to write it. Now, I am always putting myself into a "have to" frame of mind. Imagine if you "had to" reach the top. What if you became desperate to succeed?

Focus is like fire. Fire can warm you. It can cook your food or light your way or even be a place of comfort to sit around. But, only if it's under control.

If it gets out of control it can destroy everything around it. That's the same with focus. When you find yourself changing your focus with every result or setback, it gets out of control. And since you aren't focused on one destination, there's no telling where you'll end up.

The Limits Of Your Brain

While the trout is certainly limited in what it can and can't do, we have often been told that our brains are limitless in their capability. I don't believe that's true. I feel very strongly that each of us has limits. Don't get me wrong; these limits are vast but different for each of us.

I'll never cure a disease, invent a super computer, or win an Olympic event. You may never write a book, build a skyscraper, or hit a homerun in Yankee Stadium. These are limitations. But, rather than look at these as our lot in life, let's focus on what can happen.

Napoleon Hill, in his classic book, *Think And Grow Rich* states, "Whatever the mind can conceive and believe, it can achieve." Therein lies the beauty of our limitations. Whatever we can think, we have the capability of accomplishing.

If you find yourself having thoughts of building a business don't let yourself and others convince you that this is a pipedream. Dwell on the possibility and consider what steps need to be taken. Seek help and advice from those with similar successful experience. And most importantly, take action.

Your thoughts are your possibilities. What you find yourself thinking can, with effort and focus, become your reality.

The Real Difference Between You And A Trout

Trout swim. That's a fact. They also eat. These fish don't know why they do these things, they just do. Every day they face the current and keep swimming. When food passes by them, they eat. When it's time to lay eggs, they all swim to one particular spot and perform that reproductive act. Again, they don't know why. They just do.

Sometimes we can be just like trout. We often call these things habits. Routines like going to work the same way, just getting by, eating the same meal on certain days, or just living in the day to day rut can keep us from our real potential.

But, the one thing that separates us from all animals is our ability to dream. Our ability to look at possibility and imagine things getting better is the miracle that makes us human. Dreaming is what can keep us willing to go on when all seems lost. It's the possibility of success that lets us risk failure.

If an animal senses danger, it hides. It avoids any risk of harm. And, if that sense of danger persists, the animal will starve to death rather than go against its instinct for survival. Fortunately, we're different. We look at risk and either decide that it's worth pursuing, or look for ways to limit its effect.

Our greatest gift is the ability to see and choose where we end up in life. We are not limited to a certain stretch of stream to live out our lives. Our desire and willingness to keep going allows us to achieve our wildest dreams. That desire is what determines the quality of our lives.

Without dreams, we exist. Without the desire to succeed we get by. Yet, whatever our result, our choices are what determine our outcome. We decide exactly where we want to be and that's where we usually end up. For many, that concept is hard to understand, especially if they're not as successful as they'd like to be. But, the decisions or lack of decisions ultimately brought them to their destination.

The good news is that it's never too late to start dreaming about where you want to be. Regardless of your past, the future is a blank page to be colored any way you want.

Simple Succeeds

All too often we take comfort in the complex. Whenever we have a challenge or a problem that needs solving, we want our money's worth. The more complicated the answer, the better we feel. The harder it is for us to understand the answer, the more we believe it. Yet, all too often, just the opposite is true.

Let's take a look at some successes and successful people. Many times they have achieved by simplifying something. Sam Walton simplified shopping and we have Wal-Mart. Ross Perot became a billionaire by simplifying data storage. Ray Kroc simplified getting meals at McDonalds. The list goes on.

Many times when I'm interviewed, they bring up the fact that I was turned down by over 100 publishers before signing my first book contract. The question asked is how was I able to keep going through all that rejection? I always wished I had a profound, life-changing answer that would make a difference. Instead, the simple answer does. I never kept count.

I was so focused on getting one publisher to say yes to my book idea that I never counted those who said no. Each rejection letter was simply placed in a file and another proposal was sent out. My goal was to be published and not to see how many answers I could get.

Where's your focus?

"When people see an outcome that has desired results for them, they are more likely to follow direction."

10

Mending The Line

You Can't Fix The Direction Of The Stream

The bank across the stream has all the earmarks of a great holding point for fish. Everything tells you that there's a good chance of getting a real good strike if you can just keep the fly there long enough. But the current keeps moving your line and thus pulls the fly away from the target area.

You can load your line as discussed earlier in the book and then recast. The challenge there is to get the fly back to exactly where it was while avoiding getting caught in overhangs, streamside bushes, and low branches. Sometimes you can have a wind knot and end up snapping off the fly on the back cast. All of these situations mean delays. You're going to be spending too much time untangling, or retying another fly.

None of those activities can put you closer to catching a fish. Recasting is like reinventing. It may ultimately get you the end result but, based on what you've just read, is it worth the risk. There is an alternative – Mending.

Mending does what it sounds like. It corrects the location of your line without the risks of casting all over again. As the line is carried down stream it forms a bow in the middle of the current. This causes the fly to be pulled in a slanted fashion away from your target area. By simply flipping the rod as if to take the bow in the line and turn it over, you give it enough slack for the fly to remain close to where you originally cast it.

Ultimately, the more time the fly spends in the critical target area, the more opportunity for a fish to strike. Even if you avoided any of the aforementioned problems, every time you recast, you are removing the fly from the desired area and therefore lessening any chance of catching fish.

Where You've Been Determines Where You Are

Everything you've ever experienced in your life has a part in determining exactly where you are right now. What you've learned, mistakes you've made, successes you've had, as well as setbacks and disappointments you've experienced are the sum of what you've become. From here on in your life, all that's needed are adjustments rather than reconstruction.

It's like an addition on a house. When we added our great room onto our house, we did just that. Our house remained pretty much as it was before and we added all of the elements of a new room to our specifications. It looks fantastic. Now we entertain there quite often as well as enjoy family time together.

But, what if we had decided to tear down the entire house and rebuild it with the great room incorporated in the design? Wouldn't we end up with the same result? Probably. But the cost would have been astronomical, not to mention the amount of additional time involved. And with all the extra spending of time and money, we would gain nothing.

While most of you will nod your heads in agreement, my experience tells me that putting this into practice isn't as common as it should be.

Let's look at a business example that you may have actually experienced. Sales Training. All too often, sales trainers reinvent the wheel by coming up with an entirely new way of achieving sales. Everything previously put in place is eliminated for the sake of this "new" program designed to increase production.

The result is often that some people quit rather than go through another change. Most others fight the new techniques until one side or the other submits. The outcome is that the end result remains the same. The only difference is how it was achieved.

What if we took an approach similar to putting up an addition? After all, we are looking at "adding" business to what we already have.

First you need to understand all of the elements involved in reaching your current level of production. Then you look at what new levels you'd like to reach. Once you understand that, instead of spending time and money to replace the very practices that have gotten you this far, you determine the difference between where you are and where you want to be. Then you develop strategies for successfully adding the difference.

The benefits of this method is that you and your people can comfortable continue doing what has always worked and add some minor changes to get you to your new destination. Blending the old with the new will make it easier to insure cooperation of everyone involved.

Don't Add For The Sake Of Addition

When talking about making adjustments or adding ingredients, there must be a definite purpose. Having more information or more techniques does not necessarily make one better. However, making the right adjustment, saying the right thing, or adding the right benefit, can be the difference between major success and just another call.

The one critical element of constructive change is the plan. Most plans are detailed in their execution and content. The most important piece of any success plan is the outcome. When you plan for an outcome, you complete the picture. You tell yourself and others what they can expect if everything is executed properly.

This information can be the critical factor as far as who will cooperate and how dedicated they will be to this new plan. *When people see an outcome that has desired results for them, they are more likely to follow direction.* When you're making plans for yourself, having them detail the outcome will help you determine if the plan is complete or is it missing key ingredients.

Sharing what the results will be is far more important than making efforts to motivate people to carry out orders. It is important to let others see the outcome rather than just participate in the actions. Knowing the outcome will often motivate people to continue even though there may be some rough spots along the way.

On our trips to the better fishing areas we often have to hike a fairly good distance. Since these places are less traveled, there is no clear path to follow. You're jumping downed trees, fighting overgrown bushes, rocks, holes to trip in, not to mention branches in the face. Imagine how many would go through that ordeal if they didn't know what waited for them at the end of the trip.

More than likely if we were to walk without the end result being known, some would give up and others would have to rest every so often. And if we finally arrived, it might be too late in the day to fish.

But, when you know that the good fishing is at the end of this trek, you have more energy to keep going. Your patience allows you to overcome the heavy brush and difficult going. You can tell yourself that you will rest once you get there.

The difference is knowing the outcome. You don't reinvent the trip or take a different path to get to the spot. You make minor adjustments along the way. You "mend" your mental line and keep your focus on where you want to end up rather than on each and every step along the way.

"And, if I wasn't willing to take a chance on having nothing at all hit one of my flies, there was no point in even casting the line."

11

Undercuts And Snags

Don't Get Hung Up on Being Hung Up

It's often difficult to see everything below the surface of the water. Even with special sunglasses you'll miss some critical details. Add moving water to the mix and it gets even more difficult. Now imagine seeing a big trout swim by and the surrounding details become even more hidden.

You cast to where you believe the trout will see your fly. The current takes it and before you can mend or retrieve your line, it's wrapped in a clump of branches across the stream. Where's your focus?

You've got waders on so you can cross the stream, untangle your fly from the branches, cross back, and start over. That's one possibility. Do you think that great fish was watching how well you retrieved your fly? Do you think it stuck around to see if it would get another chance at your offering? Probably not. But, that wasn't your focus was it?

You concentrated on recovering your fly in a way that meant you wouldn't have to retie it. That allowed you to immediately begin fishing again which is great. But now you had no target for your fly.

What if you changed your focus for a moment? Suppose you gave yourself an out? Let's see if we can accomplish two objectives by changing focus.

As soon as you hung up on the branch, you noticed your quarry settling in to one spot. Now, you turn your focus to catching this fish and ignore the fly for now. You pull enough to snap your line and then retrieve it. You tie on a new fly without moving your location and begin casting again. This time you get the fly to go where you want and WHAM! You get the big one.

Now, after you bring your catch in to shore, guess what? You can wade across the stream, over to those branches and find the fly you snagged. You win twice.

Faith based Fishing

Fish are both predator and prey. Where I like to fish I compete with eagles and osprey. In fact, one of the great thrills is to watch these birds of prey swoop down and grab a fish. It's amazing how well they can see from the heights at which they fly.

To avoid being caught, fish hide. By staying out of sight, they get to eat another day. They also hide from their victims. Whether it's insects or small fish, trout often remain out of sight until a meal comes floating by. That means just because you can't see any fish, doesn't mean there are none around.

Streams, especially faster moving ones, have areas along the banks that have been eroded by the moving water. This wearing-away often creates an area that's shaded from the sky and darkened from the opposite shore. It's the undercut. And, it's a great place for fish to hide.

Just because you can't see them, doesn't mean they aren't there. In fact, often just the opposite is true. Trout are easily spooked. If you can see them there is a good chance they can see you. That's why we always approach a new area by staying low and out of sight. If a trout spots anything that looks like it might be a danger, they swim for cover.

That's where we want to fish. If we can put something that is attractive to a trout in an area where they feel comfortable, there's a good chance for success. Now with any success comes risk. These undercuts usually have all kinds of obstacles that can eat up your line.

But, unless you're willing to risk a few flies, or being snagged, you can't possibly expect to succeed in landing your quarry. That same holds true in business.

Most business situations are full of unknowns. In sales, you generally don't know the outcome prior to your first meeting with a prospect. You won't know how receptive someone will be to hearing about an opportunity before you talk about it. And, you'll never know how successful you can be unless and until you're willing to risk.

Growth can only come from taking risks. In business there is no status quo. You're either growing or falling behind. Maintaining one's position is nearly impossible with all of the changes happening almost instantly. For individual business owners or huge multi-national corporations, risk is the key element to growth.

As we stated earlier, you need to prepare as much as possible, gather all the information available, and then be willing to risk the possibility of failing.

Just like on this trip. I checked out and performed maintenance on all of my equipment and planned on getting to specific areas. I spoke to local experts regarding what the fish were biting on and what conditions were out there. I followed the directions to get to the best spots. I checked out the entire area for conditions, exits, and hazards.

Now, unless I was willing to risk snags there would be no fish today. Until I was willing to step into the stream even though I might fall and get soaked, there was no chance of landing a nice trout. *And, if I wasn't willing to take a chance on having nothing at all hit one of my flies, there was no point in even casting the line.*

You Need This For Your Story

If your life is a story, do you want to tell it? More importantly, is it worth listening to? It's been said that success is a journey and not a destination. I can believe that. It's always more interesting to hear what leads up to the moment of success than the success itself.

It's the details that create the excitement. You can show someone a picture of a fish you caught and get polite congratulations. Or you can share the experience of trekking through the woods and seeing a moose off to one side. You can then tell them about the majestic bald eagle perched on a high limb above you as you reached the stream. Then you can let them relive each cast with you right up until the very moment of the strike.

Your life. Is it just a still photo? Or is it a series of exciting events that everyone wants to share? Did you spend your time avoiding snags or did you cast into the undercuts with excited anticipation.

Better Not Best

If you're still not where you want to be in life or business, you need to stop what I call "Final Thinking." Final Thinking is when you end the process regardless of the result. It's when you come to the conclusion that you've done all you can and there's no hope of a successful conclusion. You start uttering "Final Phrases."

"I did my best." Have you ever said that? Think of the finality in that simple statement. How can you improve on the best? How can you expect to have success if you've already done the best you can?

What if you simply changed one word? Could you really change your perspective? I guess it depends on the word. The word I like is better. It's so flexible. It also opens your life up to possibilities.

"I did better this time." That is a statement that shows improvement. "I'll do better next time." This one is powerful. It first lets us know there is a future and that you believe you can make it better. And as long as you believe you can make things better, the future possibilities are endless.

*"Good enough
seldom is."*

12

Bends In The Rod

Hooking Is Only The Beginning

Your fly sits on the surface tied to a line that is so thin it could snap if you look at it the wrong way. Then it happens. A monster sized trout thinks your fly is the blue plate special. If you try and just pull this fish in, your line will surely snap. How can you possibly get it into your net?

It can all come down to how you hold the rod. Depending on whether you hold the tip up down or sideways will determine if the line will hold long enough to land your prize. And holding it in the right position over a long period is what it will take to succeed.

In addition to a light line, trout, even big ones, have soft mouths. Pull too hard and you'll rip the hook out. Leave too much slack or let off on your line and it could snap. Do it just right and you stand a chance of winning. But, you have to be exact. No short cuts. In this case, *good enough seldom is.*

Knowing that the line can't possibly stand the stress of the fight, you need to use leverage to spread the stress out. Your rod is the best shock absorber you have. How you hold it determines its ability to withstand the stress. When the fish is pulling away, you must hold the rod straight up in the air. This way, all of the stress is transferred to the rod alone.

The rod also becomes what the fish is fighting and will tire it out long before your line would. But the rod must be positioned properly to be effective.

Once the fish stops running, you need to begin the retrieve. You also need to be directing the fish toward where you feel the best place to land it will be. In order to do this, position the rod parallel to the water with the tip pointing in the direction you want the fish to go. Again, the rod will be doing the work.

If the fish takes off again, immediately switch the rod position to upright. You'll keep repeating this process until one of you gives in.

If I Had A Hammer

Knowing which tools to use is never enough. You need to use them. Even if you have little experience with a tool, it's still better than trying to get by without it. Imagine driving a nail into a board with your bare hands. Now imagine never having used a hammer before. Suppose you could only hit the nail every so many tries. But barehanded you could hit it every time. Which do you think would get the job done sooner?

In success there is a lot of talk about goal setting. Goals are important but not the end of the process. When you set your sights on something, the possibility of achieving it will often come down to tools and the use of them. I'll use the hammer again.

Suppose you visualize a gorgeous piece of land. It's on the beach, overlooking the mountains, or any location that is pleasing to you. You envision a magnificent house that is always filled with friends and family.

Now take the hammer, toss it on that lot and come back in a week or so. Do you think your house will be there? Of course not. Unless you're willing to pick up the tools and use them, there is no way you'll achieve your dreams.

In business you can have many tools. One of the most important ones might be someone with the talent and experience to get where you want to be. If you get the opportunity to use that tool to help you succeed, you'll not only accomplish the task at hand, but also learn from other people's experience.

Life Is Full Of Wind Knots

Even when you are totally prepared and have done everything right, outcomes aren't guaranteed. I believe the only guarantee in life is that if you do

u'll get that result – nothing. The only
...., ...id failing is to do nothing. Then you
become a failure.

What's important is that when you review the
results, you look at all the circumstances. Before
making any changes, make sure there is something
that can be changed and more important, should be.

You're out on the water and it's a breezy day. The
bugs are hatching and you feel certain that there will
be a lot of action. Cautiously you reach your spot
and begin to cast. Just as your line goes behind you a
gust of wind comes along and takes your lead and ties
it in a knot. This wind knot is now a weak spot in
your line.

You cast, lay your line down nicely, and then it
happens. A sudden rise and your fly disappears
below the surface. You lift your rod to set the hook
and suddenly your line goes limp. Snapped off right
at the wind knot. Would you change anything you've
done?

Before you answer, let me ask a different question. Can you control the wind? That wind came at
the wrong time as far as you were concerned but it
came. Nothing you could do to prevent it. Now, you
could have come later in the day and maybe the
winds would have died down. Do you suppose that
fish would wait for you?

Making changes for change's sake seldom makes
for a different result. Adjusting something you feel
you can improve is worth the effort but if something
beyond our control affects the result, it's not the time

to change your approach. You should move on and use the same approach on someone else.

If you were on the stream, you might move along to an area that is shielded from the wind by some trees. If there are fish in this spot, you can repeat everything you did exactly as before and you can expect similar success. Now, you're more likely to land that fish.

Confidence

There are certain flies with which I'm very comfortable. When I fish a new area I generally use these first because I know they catch fish. Once I've had some success, then I'll try new things to see if they work because I know there are fish present.

How do you pick comfortable flies? You choose the ones in which you have confidence. You take the lures that have worked for you under a variety of conditions and in all probability will continue doing so. But it takes time to develop this kind of comfort. You have to use them over a long period of time to know they can be trusted to produce results.

In business, you lead with what you know. Your presentation begins with things you can talk about because they've become second nature. However, you're never comfortable when you first acquire something. It takes time to make it your own.

One of my comfort phrases in a sales situation is designed to get any objections out on the table. It begins with a comfortable question, "In your opinion do you feel this program would be of value to you?" Believe it or not, I'm almost hoping they say, "No."

If they do, I respond with, "Obviously you have a reason for saying that. Do you mind if I ask what it is?" Assuming I've done a good job of explaining my offering, I always get the answer I'm looking for – the real objection. Then I focus on dealing with that concern and eventually close the sale.

Now, if I asked you to go back and read my questions and ask you to use them yourself, you may react negatively because coming from you they sound like a canned speech. Of course they do. Anything you say will sound canned until you're comfortable with it. I've made those statements thousands of times. The repetition makes it sound natural.

The key word here is repetition. Until you are willing to say it regardless of how it sounds, it will never become comfortable for you and therefore it won't produce the results.

Whether casting a fly or doing business, there is a first time for everything. By repeating it over and over, making adjustments along the way, you become a natural. Everything about you looks fluid – like you've done or said it all of your life. The key to confidence and comfort is the persistence to repeat the action or words over and over until they feel like a part of you. Then not only will you know how to do or say the right thing, but more importantly, you'll know when.

The Secret To Massive Success

Each time I sit down to write a book, I envision you, the reader. I imagine selling lots of copies and look forward to hearing how the book has impacted lives. I set a goal of selling a million books at a minimum.

Now, for those of you not familiar with the publishing industry, a million books sold is a rarity. In fact, the average book sells around a thousand copies. But, I'm not your average author. I've discovered the secret for selling a lot of books. It's the same secret for catching a lot of fish.

You have to be willing to make as many casts as it takes to catch one. Once you are willing to catch the first fish, the rest will happen. I know that sounds simple and easy to understand but too many people want to start near the end of the journey and just finish up.

You can't make a million without earning the first dollar. No one starts at $999,999 and then sets a goal of earning a dollar. You start at the beginning. And then you keep going. I know because you're reading this that I'm one book closer to a million. If it helps and you tell someone, I may get another book closer. But, unless and until I was willing to sell just one, not much will happen.

Every step you take brings you closer to your goal. Each step can produce lessons and information to make the journey go faster. Because you're willing to take as many steps as is required to reach your goal, the success you earn will last a long time.

"Only you have the final say in what you become."

13

Reflections In The Ripples

In the *New Testament* Jesus chose twelve apostles. Primarily, they were fishermen. Historically these men were generally not pillars of the community; they were not highly educated or polished in the social graces. They were as rough as their daily task required. Jesus could have had his choice of anyone He wanted for the task of spreading His word to the world. Yet He chose men from what must have been the bottom of the social ladder.

I often wondered why He did that. This trip gave me the answer. Many times, while I was casting on the rivers and streams, I would hear the phrase, "I will make you fishers of men." It would repeat itself until it almost became a distraction. Often it would seem the loudest when I came home empty handed. Finally, I have an answer that sets things straight in my mind.

If one supposes that people two thousand years ago were not flocking toward Jesus and his teachings, he needed to choose those with the qualities to stay on task for the long haul. Who better than someone whose entire lives have been made up of uncertain catches, treacherous conditions, and unpredictable outcomes. The men he chose to build his following had to endure in order to have any chance at triumph.

These men would be told to cast their "teaching nets" into other areas, yet they persevered at each location. Regardless of the size of the catch, the next day they were prepared to cast out their nets again. When the climate of those around them would turn hostile, these weathered men would stay the course. And as they proved, staying the course for as long as it takes will serve to guarantee one's arrival.

In some ways, I think that's what kept me from giving in to blowing off a day when things weren't going all that well. Ultimately, thinking of their example prevented me from giving up when the fish didn't bite or the words didn't come as fast as I thought they should have.

If this is the example that you need to get yourself going, then I'm glad to have included it in this book. I hope you enjoyed some of what preceded, but it's more important that you have something to move you to where you want to be.

I look back on each day of this adventure and am thankful for your company. In the solitude of the stream, I knew that someday we'd be together sharing my thoughts and hopefully opening your mind to the possibilities inside of you. If I have a small part in helping you take that first step, this was all worthwhile. Should our paths cross when you arrive at your destination, I'll humbly shake your hand.

For those of you who use this as leverage to begin your journey, know this. The roads will be less crowded than the streams I fish. You will find the peace of solitude and the fear of loneliness as you take each new step. You are a minority of one. Many who read this would do nothing but look back some day and wonder what could have been. You can look at a vital object – the mirror – and say you've truly lived your life.

Some of you will look at the example of the Apostles, or other successful people and think, "Not me." You may find yourself listing the limitations that may be currently keeping you back. You look at where history remembers them and fall into a dangerous practice. That of comparing.

Comparing yourself with where those people ended up and where you are now puts you at a distinct disadvantage. Often you think the result will be that you will never catch up. Consider, if you must compare, where they were when their journey started. When you study successful people, get the whole story. Many times you'll discover that massive failure and difficult setbacks plagued them until their persistence allowed them the success for which they are now known.

In my own life, those steps kept me going closer to where I wanted to end up. Had I compared myself with the great authors and speakers with whom I came in contact at the beginning, I surely would have given up, as I could never be where they were. But I listened to their stories and began thinking about what they had to overcome to get where they were. Soon it was clear that *only I had the final say in what I became.*

My whole attitude changed. Once I realized it was totally up to me to get to my destination, very little actually stood in my way. In fact, some of my largest obstacles were my own mistakes. Once I realized that I could learn from them, their size became more manageable.

I look at the fish in these steams I've visited and I see their instincts take control. Their instinct to survive is the most powerful and that's what they do – survive. I visualize you reading this book. I see some will leave me and let their survival instinct take control. When that happens, they'll get what they plan for – survival. I want more than that for my life as I hope you do as well.

Afterword – Teach A Man To Fish

Memories. Some of the best times I've had alone have been remembering different events in my life. In the silence of an empty room I've closed my eyes and relived a time when something I enjoyed happened. I could play it back in vivid detail and enjoy it as if it was happening for the first time. I think this trip will become a great memory.

Life is like a movie. Once it's lived you can look at it over and over again and enjoy any memory you choose. But, just like in the movies, someone shouts, "ACTION!" and then things need to happen. For memories to be created you must do some living. You must take action.

You can't dwell on missed opportunities but you can be ready for the next one. Crying over what might have been if only you'd taken action will only accomplish one thing. It will make certain that you'll be so wrapped up in feeling sorry for yourself that you might miss an even better opportunity for success.

Waiting for the right moment produces little in the way of success. For most worthwhile endeavors, the time will never be right. We don't know what the future holds and we aren't destined to repeat the past. What we are is right now and what we are willing to do with what we have.

People who appear to have perfect timing are often those who are constantly active and pursuing a goal. They are constantly in motion working toward their dream and because of that, good things happen.

After reading this far, you may be wondering what makes me an expert at fly-fishing and life. In either of those areas, I've got a lot to learn. But one thing I have learned and truly believe. I teach what I am most passionate about: learning. Focusing on something you want to become better at and sharing what knowledge you do have, improves you through experience and repetition. It also attracts others who can often fill in the missing pieces.

I am merely sharing my thoughts and ideas with the hopes of improving on them. My goal in bringing this to you is to make my understanding deeper and perhaps planting a seed in a future teacher who will find a better way and share it with me.

As the expression goes, "Teach a man to fish and you feed him for a lifetime." I hope I've taught one valuable lesson. My desire is to teach you the value of learning. As long as you will open your mind to the possibility of receiving something new, you will never be disappointed.

All I ask is one thing in return. If you find yourself better off because of my thoughts then I ask you to pass them along to someone you feel can benefit from them. For I believe it's true that, "No man can help another without thereby helping himself."

About John Fuhrman

John Fuhrman is the best-selling author of *Are You Living Your Dream?*; *Reject Me, I Love It*; *If They Say No Just Say Next*; and *The Credit Diet.* He has over 500,000 copies in print as well as translations in over a dozen languages around the world.

Since 1996, John has helped over 1,000,000 people through his corporate programs, convention keynotes, books, and audio programs. He has worked with companies and organizations across the US, Canada, and five former Soviet countries.

Companies engage John to help their people reach their maximum potential. More than motivational, John offers tools to help people take the necessary steps to achieve their goals and dreams.

To Learn More:
Visit www.expertspeak.com
Or call 888-883-3303
To email John:
john@expertspeak.com

For Business Lessons On The Fly

If your company, organization, or small group would like to participate in one of John's Business Learning Fly-Fishing Trips, contact him at his email. John will custom design a program and a trip on the water to increase sales or create more solid teamwork. His proven Programs can accomplish in a few days what can take months to develop. John combines fishing tips with sound advice for leaders, sales teams, and management to develop direction and to maximize potential.